Tuli Rose

Bulls, Bears, and the Baker's Bizarre Biscuits

Peek Inside

Welcome to the World of Wise Wagers and Whimsical Wealth

Hello, fearless financial adventurers, and welcome aboard the rollercoaster ride that is "Bulls, Bears and the Baker's Bizarre Biscuits." I'm thrilled to have you join me on this journey – a journey that's about to turn everything you thought you knew about investing on its head.

You're probably wondering why this book, and why now? Well, let's face it: the world of investing can often feel like a secret society where only the elite and the educated dare to tread. But I'm here to change that. I believe that everyone, yes, everyone, should have the keys to unlock the mysteries of the market. And not just the dry, textbook theories – I'm talking about the real, gritty, often-hilarious truths of investing.

"Bulls and Bears" – They're not just Wall Street mascots; they represent the highs and lows, the triumphs and tribulations of the market. But what about the baker? Ah, that's where things get interesting. The baker represents you and me – the everyday people trying to cook up some financial success in a kitchen where the recipe keeps changing.

No Jargon, Just Joy

This book is not your typical finance manual filled with jargon and graphs that make your eyes glaze over. No, this is a conversation – a fun, frank, no-holds-barred chat about money, markets, and the madness that often comes with it. It's about taking the 'boring' out of investing and adding a generous dash of joy.

Whether you're a novice investor nervously clutching your first stock certificate or a seasoned trader with scars to show for it, this book is for you. We'll start from the basics, stripping away the complexities of investing, and gradually build up to the strategies that can turn you from a market spectator to a savvy player.

The goal? Empowerment through education. I want you to close this book feeling not just informed but invigorated. I want you to look at the market and see opportunities where you once saw obstacles. I want you to understand that investing isn't just for the suit-and-tie brigade; it's for everyone – including you.

So, grab a cup of your favorite brew (and maybe a biscuit or two), settle in, and let's embark on this financial adventure together. It's going to be enlightening, it might be a bit eccentric, but I promise you – it'll be an adventure you won't forget.

Here's to turning pages, turning profits, and turning the investment world upside down. Welcome to "Bulls, Bears and the Baker's Bizarre Biscuits."

Unraveling Investment Myths: The Real Deal

Myth: Investing is a Secret Society, and You Need an Invite

Fact: Think you need a secret handshake or a decoder ring to start investing? Nope. Investing is less like an exclusive club and more like a public park. Everyone's welcome, no secret invitations required. You don't need to be a financial guru; you just need to start somewhere, anywhere.

Myth: Big Bucks Required to Board the Investment Train

Fact: Waiting to hit the financial jackpot before you invest is like waiting for rain in a desert. Start with whatever you've got in your wallet —even if it's just a few bucks. The investment train has no minimum ticket price; all aboard, penny pinchers and high rollers alike!

Myth: High Risk, High Reward: The Only Way to Sail

Fact: Betting it all on black? Slow down, cowboy. Smart investing isn't about always seeking the highest peaks; it's about not falling into valleys. Mix it up—some safe bets, some adventurous ones. It's like eating a balanced diet; you can't live on just hot sauce (no matter how much you love the thrill).

Myth: Instant Riches Just Around the Corner

Fact: If investing promised instant riches, we'd all be sipping cocktails on our yachts. Reality check: investing is more marathon than sprint. It's about making informed choices, patience, and sometimes, just sticking to it longer than your latest Netflix binge.

Myth: Your Investment Portfolio Needs Your Constant Vigilance

Fact: Gluing your eyes to stock tickers all day? That's a recipe for madness, not success. The market's mood swings are normal. Set a strategy, check in for adjustments, but don't become a helicopter parent to your investments. They need room to breathe (and grow).

Myth: Market Timing is Your Superpower

Fact: Trying to time the market perfectly is like trying to catch soap in the shower—slippery and frustrating. Instead, think rhythm, not timing. Regular, disciplined investments smooth out the market's highs and lows. It's not about the perfect moment; it's about the journey.

Myth: The Stock Market is Just Legalized Gambling

Fact: Slot machines and roulette wheels have nothing on the stock market. While both involve risk, investing is more like planting a garden than throwing dice in a casino. With gambling, it's all chance. In investing, research, strategy, and patience can tilt the odds in your favor. It's about cultivating your financial seeds with care, not hoping for a jackpot with crossed fingers.

Myth: All the Good Investment Opportunities Are Gone

Fact: Believing all the golden tickets are already taken is like saying all the great songs have been written. New opportunities are always emerging, whether it's innovative companies, industry shifts, or global trends. With a keen eye and a willingness to learn, you can spot the next big thing. Remember, every era has its breakthroughs, and yours is no exception.

Myth: Investing is Too Complicated for the Average Joe or Jane

Fact: Sure, the financial world loves its complex charts and bewildering jargon, but at its heart, investing is about making your money work for you. And guess what? You don't need a PhD in economics to achieve that. With resources aplenty and a bit of dedication to learning the basics, anyone can navigate the investment landscape. It's less about mastering every detail and more about understanding the fundamentals.

Myth: You Need a Financial Guru to Decode the Market's Mysteries

Fact: Convinced you need a high-priced financial wizard with a crystal ball to make your investment dreams come true? Think again. In today's world, armed with a wealth of information and tools at your fingertips, you can captain your own financial ship.

Diving into investing solo might seem like setting sail in uncharted waters, but with a bit of research and the plethora of free resources available, you'll soon be navigating like a seasoned explorer. Platforms and apps offer user-friendly interfaces, guiding you through investment choices with the same ease as ordering your favorite takeout.

And let's talk fees — by steering your own investment journey, you dodge the hefty charges that often come with professional advisors. These savings stay in your pocket (or, better yet, get reinvested), compounding over time. Think of it as an investment in your financial savvy. Every dollar saved on fees is a dollar that's working for you, not someone else.

So, before you hand over the wheel (and a chunk of your hard-earned cash) to someone else, consider the empowering (and cost-effective) path of DIY investing. With a bit of grit and curiosity, you'll find that you're more than capable of making informed, strategic investment decisions. Remember, in the digital age, the only real gatekeeper to the investment world is your willingness to learn and take action.

By picking up this book, you've already taken the first step. Each page you've turned is a step further away from dependency on high-fee advisors and a leap towards self-reliance in your financial decisions.

Chill Investing: The Zen of Market Swings

Here's the thing: the market's moodier than a teenager with a new TikTok account. One day it's all peace, love, and green charts; the next, it's doomscrolling through a financial apocalypse. Here's my rule — treat the market like your ex's Instagram; observe from a distance and never react in the moment. I'll teach you how to maintain your zen when the market decides to go on a rollercoaster ride, without the nausea.

Invest like the ocean: vast, deep, and unfazed by the surface storms. The stock market is a tempest, teeming with highs and lows that can tempt even the savviest investors into hasty decisions. Here's the rule: Stay calm and carry on investing. This isn't about ignoring the waves; it's about seeing through them to the calm depths below, where the true currents of wealth are steady and strong.

Here's the thing — markets swing, that's their nature. But your peace of mind? That's yours to control. Think of the market's ups and downs like weather patterns, predictable in their unpredictability. The seasoned investor knows this and plans accordingly, with a diversified portfolio that's more like a well-balanced ecosystem than a treasure chest waiting to be plundered at the first sign of gold.

The essence of chill investing lies in consistency. Regular, disciplined investments over time are your bridge over troubled waters. Dollar-cost averaging isn't just a strategy; it's your anchor. By investing a fixed amount regularly, you buy less when prices are high and more when they're low, effectively weathering the storm.

In summary, the golden rule of chill investing is simple: Stay steady. Embrace the market's moods with the serenity of a seasoned captain navigating familiar seas. Your destination?

Long-term growth and stability, reached not by chasing the winds of fortune but by setting a course that's true and holding fast to it, come what may.

Financial Wisdom: Street Smarts > Book Smarts

Forget about having a finance PhD; real financial savvy is learned in the school of hard knocks and smart savings. Ever heard of the billionaire who still clips coupons? That's the energy we're channeling. It's not about flaunting wealth, but about making smart, under-the-radar choices that pay off. I'm here to spill the secrets on how to build your empire with common sense as your foundation — no Ivy League required.

In the world of investing, it's easy to get caught up in the allure of complicated strategies and exotic investment products. But here's a secret — the most successful investors aren't necessarily the ones who understand every nuance of the market. They're the ones who apply simple, time-tested principles with consistency and discipline.

The rule here is straightforward: Financial wisdom isn't about complexity; it's about clarity and common sense. It's understanding that the path to wealth is paved with regular savings, wise spending, and investments that compound over time. It's about recognizing that the flashiest car in the parking lot probably belongs to someone who's rich on paper but poor in assets.

So how do you cultivate this street-smart financial wisdom? Start by living below your means and investing the difference. Sounds simple, but it's powerful. Embrace the basics of investing — diversify your portfolio, keep costs low, and focus on the long haul. Avoid debt like it's a crowded elevator in flu season. And remember, the goal isn't to impress your neighbors but to secure your financial future.

In essence, adopting a street-smart approach to your finances means valuing substance over style. It means making decisions based on what will bring real, lasting value to your life, not what will give you a momentary thrill. And above all, it means recognizing that the most valuable investment you can make is in your financial education.

By embracing these principles, you'll navigate the financial world with the confidence of someone who knows where they're going. You'll make smarter choices, avoid common pitfalls, and steadily build wealth over time. And when you look back on your journey, you'll realize that the real secret to financial success wasn't a secret at all — it was common sense, applied with uncommon discipline.

Your Brain on Money: Decoding Impulse Buys

2024 and our brains still haven't caught up to our tech-savvy, instant-gratification world. Why do we impulse-buy gadgets faster than downloading an app? It's your brain, tricking you into thinking you need that shiny new thing, now. Let's dive into the laughable logic behind our splurges and how pausing for a mental ad break before every purchase can save you a fortune.

It's a peculiar time to be alive. Our digital lives are a never-ending stream of 'buy now' buttons and flash sales that tap directly into our primal urge for instant satisfaction. This modern marketplace is designed to outpace our neurological firmware that once helped us survive but now tempts us into acquiring a collection of smart devices we rarely use.

Here's the rule to combat that: Embrace the Pause. Before you let that 'one-click purchase' have its way, take a breath. Picture this — each potential buy comes with a mental ad break, a momentary pause

where you question: Do I need it? Will I use it? Is there something better I could do with this money? Imagine how much clutter you'd avoid and how much fuller your savings account would look.

This isn't about denying yourself the pleasures of modern life but about upgrading your mental software to match the times. It's recognizing that not every purchase deserves your hard-earned cash. And yes, while the thrill of the buy is real, so is buyer's remorse. That's your ancient brain realizing it's been duped by shiny lights and sleek designs.

So, how do you strengthen this pause muscle? Start by tracking your impulses. Every time you resist an impulse buy, jot it down. Keep a tab on what you didn't buy, and at the end of the month, total up those savings. It's not just about the money; it's about acknowledging your power over the buy button. You might just find that the joy of saving beats the fleeting thrill of spending.

In 2024, let's not be the generation overwhelmed by impulse buys and instant regrets. Instead, let's be the savvy savers who navigate the digital bazaar with wisdom, humor, and a healthy dose of self-control. Your wallet (and future self) will thank you for it.

Investor's Brain: Unraveling Our Financial Wiring

Ever wondered why we sometimes leap before looking when it comes to money? Let's dive headfirst into the fascinating tangle of wires that is our brain, particularly when it faces the wild world of investing. You see, our noggins aren't just spongy blobs sitting in our skulls; they're like intricate circuit boards, making complex decisions about our finances, often without us realizing why we do what we do.

First up, emotions. They're like those pesky relatives who show up uninvited to your carefully planned financial party. Fear, excitement, regret – they all love to meddle in our investment plans. The trick isn't to banish them (because, let's face it, we're human, not robots); it's about managing them. Think of it as being the bouncer of your own mental soiree. When fear tries to crash your cool, calculated investment strategy, you need to check its ID at the door and say, "Not tonight, pal."

But wait, there's more. Our brains come pre-loaded with cognitive biases, sneaky little bugs in the system that can skew our financial judgment. Ever held onto a losing stock, just because you spent a lot on it? That's the sunk cost fallacy waving hello. Or how about only paying attention to info that backs up your investment choices? Say hi to confirmation bias. These biases can be as subtle as a whisper but as impactful as a bull in a china shop when it comes to your money.

Now, here's the game-changer: awareness. By simply knowing about these emotional gatecrashers and cognitive gremlins, you're already on your way to smarter investing. It's like having a map in a maze; you might still hit a few dead ends, but you're way more likely to find the treasure. So, as we navigate this brainy jungle of investing, remember, the goal isn't to outsmart the market; it's to outsmart our own wonderfully weird, wonderfully human brains.

The Stealth Wealth Formula: Flashy is Passé

Ever noticed how in movies, the truly rich guy is never the one flashing cash at every turn, but rather the unassuming character who owns the place? That's stealth wealth. It's about being the financial ninja: all the wealth, none of the show-off. In an age where social media flaunts every purchase, stealth wealth is the art of being rich without needing to prove it to the world. It's financial strength whispering instead of shouting.

Here's a fact: real wealth isn't loud. It's quiet, patient, and incredibly wise. It understands that the most powerful statement you can make is none at all. Why? Because when you're genuinely wealthy, you don't need external validation. Your bank account, investments, and freedom speak volumes, in hushed tones only you need to hear.

So, how do you embrace this ninja way? First, live below your means. It's not about self-denial but about smart allocation. Why buy a flashy car on loan when you can invest that money and buy it outright later — if you still want it? Stealth wealth is about choices, not sacrifices. It's choosing to invest rather than impress.

Next, focus on building assets, not liabilities. Every dollar you spend on something that depreciates is a dollar not spent on building your empire. Stealth wealth champions know this. They buy assets that grow over time—stocks, bonds, real estate. These are the invisible bricks of your financial fortress.

And remember, stealth wealth is also about protection. It's about having the financial backup to say no to things that don't serve you and yes to the things that do. This financial buffer gives you the freedom to make choices based on what you truly value, not what you're supposed to value according to society's flashy standards.

In 2024, let's redefine wealth. Let it not be measured by the brands you wear or the car you drive, but by the choices you can afford to make and the peace of mind those choices bring. Stealth wealth isn't just a financial strategy, it's a lifestyle — one that values substance over appearance, and long-term fulfillment over short-term gratification.

Embrace the stealth wealth formula: be the master of your finances, not a billboard for consumption. Let your wealth be a quiet testament to your savvy, your discipline, and your understanding that true richness is found in the life you lead, not the things you own.

Dividends: The Unsung Heroes of Investing

Let's talk about dividends, the unsung heroes in the world of investing. Think of dividends as your investments' way of saying "Thanks for believing in us!" It's like getting a pat on the back, but instead of a pat, you get cash. And who doesn't like a little extra cash?

What's a Dividend, Anyway?

For the uninitiated, dividends are payments that companies make to their shareholders out of their profits. It's like getting a slice of the profit pie just because you own a piece of the company. The beauty of dividends is their simplicity – you invest in a dividend-paying stock, and voilà, you get regular payments just for holding on to it.

But here's where it gets interesting. Dividends can be reinvested to buy more shares, leading to more dividends, which can then buy even more shares. It's a beautiful cycle that's all about compounding. Over time, this can turn your investments from a trickle into a roaring stream. Think of it as planting a seed and watching it grow into a mighty tree, all from the power of reinvesting those dividends.

Now, before you jump headfirst into the dividend pool, remember, not all dividend stocks are created equal. Some companies offer high dividends to attract investors, but if their profits aren't stable, those dividends might as well be written in sand. Look for companies with a track record of not just paying dividends but consistently increasing them. Stability is key here.

In the rollercoaster world of investing, dividends are like the steady Eddies. They offer a semblance of stability in an otherwise unpredictable market. While they might not have the allure of skyrocketing stocks, they provide a steady, predictable income stream. And in times of market turmoil, that predictability is worth its weight in gold.

So, the golden rule with dividends? Diversify and reinvest. Don't put all your eggs in one basket, and use those dividends to fuel further growth. It's a strategy that may not make headlines, but in the long run, it's a smart way to build and sustain your wealth.

Financial FOMO: The Fear of Missing Out on Million$

Ever felt that itch when you hear about someone making a fortune overnight in the stock market? That's Financial FOMO — the fear of missing out on potential millions. It's the modern gold rush, but instead of pickaxes and pans, we're armed with apps and alerts, constantly bombarded with stories of meteoric rises and instant wealth. Here's the rule to combat that: Invest with intention, not impulse.

Financial FOMO can lead even the wisest among us down the path of risky bets and speculative ventures. It whispers seductively about the next big thing, urging us to jump in before it's too late. But here's the twist: for every overnight success, there are countless untold stories of loss, regret, and what-ifs.

To steer clear of FOMO's siren call, anchor yourself to a well-thought-out investment strategy. This isn't about turning your back on opportunities; it's about recognizing which opportunities align with your goals and risk tolerance. It's choosing to be the tortoise in a world that glorifies the hare.

Start by setting clear, personal investment goals. Are you saving for a home, planning for retirement, or building an emergency fund? Your goals should dictate your investment choices, not the fear of missing out on the latest trend. Next, diversify your portfolio. Putting all your eggs in one basket is not just risky; it's a recipe for financial heartbreak. A diversified portfolio helps buffer against the volatility of the market and FOMO-driven decisions.

Most importantly, educate yourself. Understanding the basics of investment can immunize you against FOMO. Knowledge is power — the power to make informed decisions, to sift through the noise, and to invest in a way that's right for you, not just because it's trending on social media.

Embrace a mindset of abundance, not scarcity. The market will always have opportunities; missing one isn't the end of your financial journey but a step towards a more mindful and deliberate investment path. Remember, true wealth is built over time, through patience, discipline, and a keen eye for the right opportunity — not just any opportunity that comes knocking.

Investing with intention transforms Financial FOMO from a source of anxiety into a reminder of your financial savvy and discipline. It's about making the market work for you, on your terms, according to your timeline. That's how you turn the fear of missing out into the joy of missing nothing at all.

The Greenback Diet: Trimming the Financial Fat

In a world where consumerism is king, and the latest gadget is just a credit card swipe away, financial health often falls by the wayside. Yet, the secret to building lasting wealth isn't in earning more — it's in optimizing what you have.

The rule: eliminate excess; optimize essentials.

Think of your finances as your diet. Just as empty calories can sabotage your health goals, frivolous spending can undermine your financial well-being.

The Greenback Diet is about trimming the financial fat — cutting out unnecessary expenses and focusing on what truly adds value to your life. It starts with a thorough audit of your spending. Track every dollar for a month, and you'll likely discover that the little things — daily coffees, unused subscriptions, impulse buys — add up to a significant amount.

Next, categorize your expenses into 'needs' and 'wants.' Needs are non-negotiable: rent, groceries, utilities. Wants are everything else. This doesn't mean eliminating all your wants; it means being intentional about them. Budget for enjoyment, but ensure it's within your means and doesn't detract from your financial goals.

Now, focus on optimizing your essentials. Can you negotiate a better rate on your bills? Is there a more cost-effective grocery store? Small optimizations can lead to big savings over time, freeing up more money to invest in your future.

Finally, apply the savings to your financial goals. Increase your emergency fund, pay down debt, invest in your future. Every dollar you redirect from frivolous spending to your

goals accelerates your journey to financial
independence.

The Greenback Diet isn't about deprivation; it's
about prioritization. It's recognizing that true
financial freedom comes not from the next
purchase but from the peace of mind knowing
you're living

within your means, investing in your future,
and focusing on what truly matters.

Detective Investing: The Case of the Hidden Gems

Investing isn't just about following the crowd to the latest hot stock; it's about being a detective, searching for clues that lead to hidden gems. These are the investments not yet on everyone's radar, offering potential for significant returns before they become the talk of the town.

Becoming a successful detective investor means doing your homework. The rule is to look beyond the spotlight; treasure often lies hidden. It involves digging into financial statements, understanding market trends, and spotting opportunities that others overlook. It's not about having insider information but about having an insider's curiosity and an outsider's perspective.

Start by exploring sectors that are out of favor but poised for recovery. Look for companies with strong fundamentals — solid balance sheets, consistent cash flow, and competitive advantages — that are undervalued by the market. These are your hidden gems, waiting to be discovered and polished to reveal their true value.

Remember, the most lucrative investments are often the ones no one is talking about yet. By the time a stock is headline news, you've likely missed the window of opportunity for the highest gains. So, keep your ear to the ground, stay patient, and when you find a hidden gem, be ready to act before it catches the spotlight.

In the end, detective investing isn't just about finding undervalued stocks; it's about adopting a mindset of curiosity, diligence, and foresight. It's a commitment to looking beyond the obvious, seeking out potential in places others have disregarded. This approach doesn't just lead to financial rewards; it makes the investment journey an engaging and intellectually stimulating adventure.

Embrace the Chaos: Market Unpredictability for Dummies

In the dance of dollars and digits that defines our markets, unpredictability plays the lead. It twirls and leaps in patterns that even the keenest minds find baffling at times. This dance floor, where fortunes are both made and lost, isn't for the faint-hearted. But here's the insider tip: thriving in this chaos isn't about predicting the next big move; it's about building resilience and flexibility into your financial strategy.

Imagine navigating a maze that constantly shifts around you. The exit might change, but your ability to adapt keeps you moving forward. That's the essence of embracing market unpredictability. It's understanding that while we can't control the market's moods, we can control our reactions to them. This isn't about a crystal ball that shows us the future but about a compass that keeps us oriented towards our long-term goals, regardless of the storms we face.

The real skill lies in crafting a portfolio that's both sturdy and nimble — diverse enough to withstand market gyrations and agile enough to capitalize on opportunities as they arise. Think of it as financial judo; using the market's momentum to your advantage. When others panic, your cool head and strategic positioning allow you to see clearly and act decisively.

Moreover, this approach demystifies the market's chaos, transforming what seems like a random walk down Wall Street into a deliberate journey towards financial empowerment. Yes, the market will test your resolve with its capricious ways. But with a plan that accounts for unpredictability, you turn potential pitfalls into stepping stones towards your financial aspirations.

In essence, the chaos isn't a bug of the financial markets; it's a feature. By accepting and preparing for it, you not only safeguard your investments but also set the stage for growth that outpaces the tumult. It's a reminder that in the realm of investing, the only certainty is uncertainty itself — and mastering your response to it is the ultimate investment in your financial future.

Mastering the Market: Game Theory in Investing

Imagine the stock market as a giant chessboard where every move you make influences and is influenced by the moves of others. This isn't just investing; it's strategic gameplay, where understanding your opponents – in this case, other investors – can make or break your success. Welcome to Game Theory in investing, where every decision is a calculated step in an intricate dance of dollars and sense.

Reading the Room: Predicting Market Moves

In the world of Game Theory, predicting your opponent's next move is crucial. In the stock market, this translates to anticipating how other investors will react to market trends, news, and global events. It's like trying to guess your friend's next move in a game of rock-paper-scissors, but with your hard-earned cash at stake. Will they panic sell at the first sign of trouble, or hold steady through the storm? Understanding these patterns can give you a strategic edge.

Nash Equilibrium: Finding Your Financial Sweet Spot

John Nash, a rockstar in the Game Theory world, introduced the concept of Nash Equilibrium – a state where no player can benefit by changing their strategy if others keep theirs unchanged. In investing, this is your 'sweet spot.' It's about finding a balance in your portfolio where you're not constantly reacting to every market hiccup. Stick to your strategy, and let the market players do their thing.

Zero-Sum Games: Your Loss, Their Gain

In some investments, particularly in short-term trading, the scenario is often a zero-sum game. Picture a pie – if someone takes a bigger slice, that means less for everyone else. Quick wins can be tempting, but they often mean someone else is losing out. Long-term investing, however, opens the door to non-zero-sum games, where everyone can get a bigger slice of the pie over time.

Playing the Long Game: Strategy Over Impulse

The key takeaway from Game Theory in investing? Think long-term and strategic. Impulsive decisions based on short-term market fluctuations are like blind moves in a chess game. Instead, plan your moves, anticipate market trends and investor behaviors, and stay focused on your endgame.

Checkmate: Your Winning Move in the Market

By applying Game Theory to your investment strategy, you're not just throwing darts in the dark; you're playing a calculated game of financial chess. And in this game, patience, strategy, and understanding the psychology of other players can lead you to that satisfying checkmate – a robust and thriving investment portfolio.

Money's Bizarre Adventure: Everyday Economics

Navigating the world of economics is akin to wandering through a carnival funhouse — distorted mirrors, unexpected turns, and all. It's a bizarre adventure, where the rules of everyday life twist and stretch in surprising ways. Here's the straight shot: understanding the quirks of economics isn't just for academics or Wall Street wizards; it's essential for anyone looking to navigate the financial funhouse with their wallet intact.

Consider the seemingly simple act of buying a coffee. In the realm of everyday economics, this purchase is a web of supply and demand, cost versus benefit, and opportunity costs. The price you pay isn't just about beans and labor; it's a dance of market forces, from the farmer to the barista. And the choice to buy that coffee? It's an economic decision, weighing the joy of your morning brew against what else those dollars could do for you.

This bizarre adventure doesn't stop at the coffee shop. It extends to every corner of your financial life, from deciding to take a job, to choosing a savings account, to investing in the stock market. Each decision is a mini-lesson in economics, a practical application of theories that might seem dry or distant in a textbook.

Here's the practical tip: start seeing these economic principles in action in your daily life. When you're faced with a financial decision, big or small, take a moment to consider the underlying economics. What's the opportunity cost of this choice? How does supply and demand factor in? By applying these concepts, you'll start to see the economic funhouse for what it is—a series of predictable patterns and principles that, once understood, can be navigated to your advantage.

Remember, economics isn't just about money; it's about how we make choices in a world of limited resources. By embracing the bizarre adventure of everyday economics, you equip yourself with the knowledge to make smarter, more informed decisions. It's about turning the economic funhouse mirrors straight, seeing the world of finance as I truly is, and using that clarity to chart a course towards your financial goals.

In essence, Money's Bizarre Adventure is your invitation to peel back the curtain on the economic wizardry of daily life. It's about transforming the seemingly complex and confusing into something understandable and actionable. With this practical, straightforward approach, you're not just surviving the economic funhouse; you're mastering it, one decision at a time.

Tortoise Investing: Wins the Race

Forget the flash-in-the-pan success stories you hear now and then, where someone strikes it rich overnight in the stock market. Real, sustainable investing is more tortoise than hare; it's about steady progress, not sudden sprints. The golden rule? Patience pays off. In the world of investing, slow and steady does indeed win the race.

Here's the deal: the market is a wild beast, prone to leaps and lunges. But remember Aesop's fable — the tortoise, with its unwavering determination, ultimately outpaces the hare. Investing is similar. It's the consistent, disciplined approach that leads to long-term success, not the erratic jumps at every so-called opportunity.

Consider this: compounding interest, the investor's best friend. It's the magic that happens when your investments earn returns, and those returns earn returns of their own. But here's the catch — it takes time. Like a fine wine, the true power of compounding interest is only revealed with age. This is where the tortoise investors shine. They understand that by sticking to their investment strategy, even when the market dips, they're setting themselves up for significant growth down the line.

So, how do you adopt this tortoise investing strategy? Start with a clear, long-term investment plan. Identify your financial goals — retirement, a dream home, your children's education — and tailor your investment strategy to meet those objectives. Diversify your portfolio to spread the risk, and then, perhaps most importantly, stay the course. Market volatility can be nerve-wracking, but remember, the tortoise investor doesn't flinch at the first sign of trouble.

Here's a practical tip: automate your investments. Set up regular contributions to your investment accounts, so you're consistently investing, come rain or shine. This not only disciplines your investing approach but also takes advantage of dollar-cost averaging, buying more shares when prices are low and fewer when they're high.

In essence, embracing the tortoise mentality in investing is about recognizing the value of time. It's understanding that while the market's swings might tempt you into hasty decisions, true wealth is built through persistence, patience, and a keen eye on the horizon. Be the tortoise, and let time be your ally on the journey to financial prosperity.

Side Hustle to Main Hustle: Investing in Yourself

In a world obsessed with side hustles, let's flip the script. Instead of spreading yourself thin across a myriad of gigs, consider the most lucrative investment you can make: pouring into yourself.

Remember! your greatest asset is you. invest accordingly.

Yes, diversifying income streams is wise, but nothing beats the returns on investing in your own skills, knowledge, and personal growth.

Here's the kicker: every skill you learn, every bit of knowledge you acquire, and every experience you gain adds compound interest to your personal and professional worth. This isn't just about boosting your resume; it's about enhancing your ability to navigate and excel in an ever-changing world. The market values rarity and expertise — become rare, become an expert, and watch your value soar.

So, how do you transform your side hustle into your main hustle? Start with passion. What drives you? What do you love doing so much that time flies when you're immersed in it? That's your starting point. Next, level up your skills in that area. Online courses, workshops, books, mentorships — resources abound for those willing to seek them out. Remember, the most successful people are lifelong learners; they never stop growing.

Embrace the entrepreneurial spirit. Your side hustle isn't just a job; it's a testing ground for your business acumen. Treat it as a mini-MBA. Learn about marketing, sales, customer service, and finance. These skills are invaluable, whether you're scaling your own business or climbing the corporate ladder.

Networking is non-negotiable. Connect with others in your field. Share your knowledge and learn from theirs. Opportunities often come from the most unexpected places, and a strong network is a safety net for the entrepreneurial high wire.

Finally, don't fear failure. See it as tuition for the most personalized course you'll ever take — life. Each setback is a lesson, honing your resilience and preparing you for the next challenge. The path from side hustle to main hustle is rarely linear, but every step forward is a step toward the ultimate investment in yourself.

In essence, shifting the focus from external side hustles to the internal hustle of self-improvement and personal investment is a game-changer. It's a journey that requires patience, persistence, and a willingness to bet on yourself. But remember, in the economy of life, you're the blue-chip stock. Invest in yourself, and the dividends will be life-changing.

The Financial Time Machine: Investing with Hindsight

Rule alarm: Past performance is not an indicator of future results, but it can be a teacher.

If only we had a financial time machine, right? Imagine hopping back for a quick chat with your younger self, armed with the investment knowledge you have now. While we can't turn back the clock, we can use the past as a powerful learning tool to shape a smarter financial future.

Here's the reality: the market has cycles, and while history doesn't repeat itself, it often rhymes. The crashes, the booms, and the seemingly unpredictable swings — all have lessons hidden within them. The savvy investor knows to look back not in regret but for insight. It's about understanding the signals, recognizing patterns, and learning from those who navigated similar waters before us.

Investing with hindsight isn't about wishing you'd made different choices; it's about applying the wisdom gained from those choices moving forward. Start by reviewing your investment history. What worked? What didn't? More importantly, why? This retrospective analysis is your groundwork for developing a more informed, resilient investment strategy.

Embrace the long view. Short-term market movements are noise, distractions that can lead you off course. The long view is your financial compass, guiding you towards decisions that align with your ultimate goals, not the fleeting trends of the moment.

Diversification is your time machine's safety mechanism. By spreading your investments across different asset classes, you're not just protecting yourself from volatility; you're ensuring that parts of your portfolio can benefit from future opportunities you might not yet see.

Finally, cultivate a mindset of continuous learning. The most successful investors are perpetual students of the market. They read, they question, they seek understanding — not just for the next investment, but for the lifelong journey of financial growth and security.

In essence, while we may not have a financial time machine, we do have something just as valuable: the ability to learn from the past to inform our future. It's about leveraging hindsight as foresight, turning every experience into a stepping stone towards financial wisdom and success.

Cash Cushions: Building Your Financial Safety Net

Ever been caught off-guard by an unexpected expense? Welcome to life! It throws curveballs, and while we can't predict them all, we can certainly prepare. Let's get real, money in the bank beats wishful thinking. That's where the cash cushion comes into play. Think of it like your financial shock absorber — it softens the blow of life's surprises without derailing your financial train.

Here's the deal: having a cash cushion isn't about hoarding money under your mattress. It's about smart financial preparedness. Start with an emergency fund. This isn't your vacation fund or the new gadget savings; it's your "Oh no, my car just broke down" fund. How much do you need? A good rule of thumb is three to six months' worth of living expenses. It sounds like a chunk, but it's your financial lifeline when things go sideways.

How do you build this fund? First, look at your budget. Find areas where you can cut back — maybe that daily coffee run or eating out less. Next, set up a dedicated savings account for your emergency fund. Treat it like a bill; automate your savings so a portion of your paycheck goes directly into this account. Even small amounts add up over time.

Remember, the goal here isn't to live on a financial knife-edge, saving so aggressively that you can't enjoy life. It's about finding a balance — saving enough to give you peace of mind but still enjoying the present.

This cash cushion does more than just cover unexpected expenses. It gives you freedom—the freedom to make choices without financial pressure, the freedom to take calculated risks, and, most importantly, the freedom to sleep soundly at night, knowing you're covered.

And when life inevitably happens, and you need to dip into your emergency fund, don't beat yourself up. That's what it's there for. Just focus on rebuilding it, one dollar at a time, once the crisis has passed.

In essence, your cash cushion is the foundation of your financial health. It's the first step towards building a resilient, flexible financial future. So start today, even if it's just a few dollars at a time. Your future self will thank you for it, trust me.

The No-Sweat Investment Strategy

Alright, let's cut to the chase. You want to grow your money without turning investing into your second job. I get it. So, here's the down-and-dirty guide to investing with minimal effort and maximum chill.

Rule: Keep It Brain-Dead Simple

Investing isn't quantum physics, despite what those finance gurus want you to think. Your game plan? Index funds and ETFs. Why? Because they spread your risk by investing in a bunch of companies at once. Pick one that matches how gutsy you feel about your money and how long you're willing to let it ride.

Automation is your best buddy. Direct a part of your paycheck straight to your investment account. It's like you're making money without even trying. Thanks to the wonder of compounding, your stash grows over time, all by itself.

The financial world loves drama. My advice? Ignore it. Markets go up, markets go down – it's their thing. Stick to your plan. Jumping on every "hot tip" or panic selling at every dip is a surefire way to mess up.

Annual Check-Up, Not Daily Obsession

Look, I'm not saying ignore your investments completely. Glance at them once a year to make sure they're still doing their thing. It's like checking if your car needs an oil change, not watching it like a hawk every time you hit the road.

Here's the kicker: being a lazy investor doesn't mean you don't care about your money. It means you're smart enough to let it grow without fussing over it daily. Stick to these principles, and watch your money work for you, not the other way around.

A Note from the Author:

As we dive into the simplicity of the "No-Sweat Investment Strategy," I want to pause and reflect on the journey we've undertaken together through the pages of this book. We've navigated the nuanced terrains of investing, armed with tools, strategies, and insights aimed at empowering you, the reader, to make informed financial decisions.

This chapter, with its emphasis on a laid-back approach to investing, might seem like a departure from the proactive, hands-on strategies we've explored. However, it's a testament to the book's core philosophy: that there's no one-size-fits-all solution in investing. Just as a tailor adjusts a suit to fit its wearer perfectly, so too must our investment strategies be tailored to fit our individual lives, goals, and comfort levels.

Investing doesn't have to be a constant hustle. For some, the beauty of investing lies in its simplicity and the peace of mind that comes with knowing your finances are growing steadily, without the need for daily intervention. This chapter is a nod to those who prefer the scenic route on their financial journey, proving that sometimes, less can indeed be more.

As we move forward, remember that the diversity of strategies presented in this book is designed to equip you with a broad spectrum of options. Whether you're meticulously analyzing stocks, exploring the wonders of compound interest, or setting your investments on cruise control, the key is to find the rhythm that resonates with you. Investing is as much about understanding the markets as it is about understanding yourself.

Let this chapter serve not as a contradiction, but as a complement to the rich tapestry of advice we've woven together. In the end, the choice of how actively you engage with your investments is yours — a choice that should align with your lifestyle, goals, and the legacy you wish to build.

As we turn the page to explore a more hands-on approach to investing, it's crucial to remember that active investing isn't just about keeping busy; it's about being smart and tactical with your financial decisions. For those of you who find thrill in the chase and satisfaction in the strategy, the next chapter is your playground.

Remember - it's your life, your choices, and you can do whatever you're comfortable with. I'm here to guide you on how to fish, not to serve you the meal. Whether you're casting your line in tranquil waters or navigating the rapid streams, the skills you develop will serve you in all facets of your financial journey. Let's dive into the dynamic world of active investing with an open mind and a keen eye for opportunity.

Financial Fitness Bootcamp: No Sweat Guide to Bulking Up Your Wallet

Rule: keep it simple, smarty. Investing isn't rocket science, it's common sense on steroids.

Welcome to the only bootcamp where the only thing heavy lifting is your wallet. Think of this as your laid-back, no-nonsense guide to making your money work harder than a caffeinated squirrel before winter. Let's cut through the financial jargon and get straight to the point: making your investments as effortlessly cool as a cucumber in a freezer.

Step 1: The Portfolio Selfie

Let's start with a quick snapshot of where you're at. Spread out your investments and take a good, hard look. What's looking back at you? A mishmash of "meh" or some solid gold? It's time to Marie Kondo your portfolio. If it doesn't spark joy (or profits), thank it for its service and say goodbye.

Step 2: Mix It Up

Diversification is just a fancy way of saying, "Don't put all your eggs in one basket." Why? Because if that basket takes a tumble, you're going to have a bad time. Spread your investments across different types—stocks, bonds, maybe a sprinkle of real estate or a pinch of crypto. It's like creating the perfect playlist for a road trip; you need variety to keep it interesting.

Step 3: Steady as She Goes

The secret sauce? Consistency. Investing regularly is like eating your veggies or brushing your teeth — it's good for you, and it adds up over time. Automate your investments like you do your bill payments. It's the "set it and forget it" of growing your wealth. Before you know it, you'll be seeing those numbers climb.

Step 4: Know When to Hold 'Em

The market's going to go up and down, and that's okay. The key is not to panic sell the moment things look shaky. It's about playing the long game. Think of it as riding out the waves on a surfboard. Stay balanced, keep your eyes on the horizon, and enjoy the ride.

Step 5: Safety Net

Just like in any good workout routine, you need to ensure you're not going to injure yourself. Financially, this means having an emergency fund and the right insurances in place. It's not the most exciting part of financial planning, but it's what keeps you in the game when life throws a curveball.

The Cool Down

There you have it — your no-sweat guide to financial fitness. Remember, it's all about making smart, consistent choices that align with your goals. There's no need to complicate things. Keep it simple, stay the course, and watch your financial health improve step by step. You've got this!

The No-BS Glossary of Investment Terms

Bear Market: Not a market selling large, furry creatures. It's when stock prices are falling faster than your dropped ice cream cone, signaling pessimism and a bit of doom and gloom. Picture a bear swiping down—those are your stocks, going down.

Bull Market: The opposite of a bear market. Here, prices charge up like a bull with its horns aimed high. It's all about optimism, energy, and investors doing a happy dance because everything's going up, including spirits (and hopefully, your portfolio).

Compound Interest: Think of it as your money making babies, and those babies making more babies, and so on. It's the snowball effect with your cash. Start small, roll it down the financial hill, and watch it grow into a massive snow boulder.

Diversification: Don't put all your eggs in one basket. Spread 'em out. If one basket falls, you're not going to brunch empty-handed. It's about mixing up your investments to reduce risk. Stocks, bonds, real estate — get a slice of each pie.

ETF (Exchange-Traded Fund): Imagine a basket. Inside this basket, there's a mix of investments — stocks, bonds, maybe some gold. Now, sell pieces of this basket on the stock market. That's an ETF. It's like a party platter for investors: a little bit of everything in one purchase.

Liquidity: How quickly you can turn your investments into cold, hard cash without losing value. High liquidity means you can sell it fast (like a hot cake). Low liquidity means it's a slow mover (like that weird knick-knack at your garage sale).

Portfolio: This is your investment collection — not photos, but stocks, bonds, ETFs, maybe some crypto. It's everything you've invested in, sitting pretty in your financial album.

Volatility: Think of it as the mood swings of the market. One day it's up, the next day it's down. It's the rollercoaster ride that can make or break your stomach (and your investments).

Yield: This is what your investment pays you for owning it, like interest on a savings account or dividends from stocks. High yield, more money in your pocket; low yield, well, it's better than nothing.

Zombie Stock: A stock that's not quite dead but not exactly alive and thriving. It's wandering the market aimlessly, not growing, just existing. Like a zombie, it's kind of spooky and probably best avoided.

Alpha: This isn't just the first letter of the Greek alphabet or what your dog thinks you are. In the investing world, alpha is all about outperforming. It's the extra return on your investment that makes you strut like a peacock because you beat the market. Go ahead, wear those feathers proudly.

Beta: Not to be confused with the second-in-command to the alpha wolf, beta in finance measures how much your investments are likely to boogie with the market. High beta? Your stocks are dancing in sync with the market's ups and downs. Low beta? They're chilling out, doing their own thing, regardless of the market's drama.

Hedge Fund: Picture a hedge, but instead of being made of shrubs, it's made of cash. These funds are like the ninjas of the investment world, using sophisticated strategies to protect against market downturns (hence the "hedge"). But watch out, they often come with ninja-level fees and are usually invitation-only, like that exclusive club you always wanted to sneak into.

IPO (Initial Public Offering): This is when a company decides it's ready to take its relationship with the public to the next level by selling shares on the stock market for the first time. It's the financial equivalent of a debutante ball, where a company goes from private to public, trading its private, quiet life for the spotlight and paparazzi of Wall Street.

Market Capitalization: Imagine if you could put a price tag on a company, capturing its total value in a single number. That's market cap. It's like weighing a giant pumpkin at the fair; the heavier it is (or the higher the market cap), the more significant (and potentially impactful) the company is in the market.

P/E Ratio (Price-to-Earnings Ratio): Think of this as the price tag for a piece of a company's future earnings. It tells you how much investors are willing to pay for every dollar a company earns. A high P/E might mean the stock is overvalued, like paying gourmet prices for fast food. A low P/E could be a bargain, or it could be a lemon at a discount. Shopper beware.

REIT (Real Estate Investment Trust): Imagine owning a slice of a shopping mall, an office building, or an apartment complex without having to fix toilets or chase down rent. That's what REITs offer— a way to invest in real estate and earn dividends without getting your hands dirty. It's like Monopoly, but with real money and no jail time.

Short Selling: This is the financial equivalent of betting that a stock's price will fall. You borrow shares, sell them at today's price, and hope to buy them back cheaper later. It's like selling your friend's PS5 while they're on vacation, planning to replace it with a cheaper one before they get back. High risk, potentially high reward, but ethically murky and not for the faint-hearted.

Rally: This isn't about cars zooming through dirt roads but about stock prices speeding upwards, often faster than a kid chasing an ice cream truck. It's when the market or a specific stock takes a joyride, and prices climb higher, making investors cheer louder than fans at a football game.

Index Fund: Picture a shopping basket, but instead of groceries, you're buying a little piece of every stock in a particular market index, like the S&P 500. It's the investment equivalent of buying the entire buffet — it offers a taste of everything, reducing the risk of indigestion if one dish turns out to be less appetizing.

Junk Bonds: Don't let the name fool you; these aren't worthless. They're just riskier than your average bond, offering higher interest rates to make up for that risk. Think of them as the daredevils of the bond world, walking the tightrope without a net. Exciting, yes, but not for the faint of heart.

Quantitative Easing: This is when central banks, like financial wizards, conjure money out of thin air, aiming to stimulate the economy. They use this magic money to buy bonds, lowering interest rates, and making it easier for businesses and individuals to borrow and spend. It's like economic caffeine, intended to perk things up when the economy starts snoozing.

Robo-Advisor: Imagine a robot giving you investment advice, but instead of a cold, metal buddy, it's sophisticated software that manages your investments using algorithms. It's like having a financial GPS that keeps you on the best route to your financial goals, minus the backseat driving.

Stop-Loss Order: This is your financial safety net. It's an order to sell a stock if it falls to a certain price, stopping the bleeding before it becomes a hemorrhage. Think of it as the bungee cord that snaps you back before you hit the ground on a financial free fall.

Frequently Asked Questions About Investing

I'm new to investing. Where should I start?

Start with the basics — understand your financial goals and risk tolerance. Educate yourself about different types of investments (stocks, bonds, mutual funds, etc.) and consider starting with a low-cost, diversified index fund. Remember, investing is a marathon, not a sprint.

How much money do I need to start investing?

The good news is you don't need a fortune to start investing. Many online platforms allow you to start with a small amount, even as little as $50. The key is to start early and invest consistently, no matter the amount.

Should I invest in stocks or mutual funds?

It depends on your investment goals and risk tolerance. Stocks can offer higher returns but come with higher risk. Mutual funds provide diversification and are managed by professionals, which might suit you if you prefer a more hands-off approach.

How do I deal with market volatility?

Market swings are a normal part of investing. Stay focused on your long-term goals, avoid making decisions based on short-term market movements, and maintain a diversified portfolio to cushion against volatility.

What's the difference between active and passive investing?

Active investing involves frequent buying and selling of stocks to beat the market performance, whereas passive investing involves a long-term, buy-and-hold strategy, typically in index funds, mirroring market performance.

How often should I check my investments?

Resist the urge to check your investments daily. Quarterly or bi-annual reviews are sufficient unless there are significant market changes. Over-monitoring can lead to impulsive decisions.

Can I invest if I have debts?

It's advisable to pay off high-interest debts first, like credit card debt, as the interest can outpace any potential investment returns. However, if you have low-interest debt, you can balance debt repayment with investing.

What is dollar-cost averaging, and should I use it?

Dollar-cost averaging means investing a fixed amount regularly, regardless of market conditions. It reduces the impact of market volatility and can be a smart strategy for long-term investors.

How important is diversification?

Diversification is crucial. It involves spreading your investments across different assets to reduce risk. Don't put all your eggs in one basket — mix it up with stocks, bonds, real estate, and international investments.

When's the right time to sell my investments?

Consider selling if your investment goals or timeline changes, or if an asset consistently underperforms. However, remember to think long-term and avoid reacting to short-term market fluctuations.

Is it better to invest in individual stocks or ETFs?

ETFs (Exchange-Traded Funds) offer diversification and are generally less risky than individual stocks. However, individual stocks can offer higher rewards (and risks). It's like choosing between a buffet (ETFs) or ordering a single dish (stocks) – both have their perks, depending on your appetite for risk and variety.

How important is it to understand market trends?

Understanding market trends is like being able to read the weather before a sailing trip. It helps you navigate and make informed decisions. However, don't get too caught up in short-term trends; focus on the long-term horizon.

What should I do when a stock I own plummets?

When a stock plummets, first, don't panic. Assess the situation – is it a temporary dip or a sign of long-term trouble? Review the company's fundamentals and decide whether it aligns with your investment strategy. Sometimes the best action is no action.

How can I learn more about investing?

The world of investing is vast. Start with reliable books and financial websites. Consider attending workshops or online courses. And remember, experience is a great teacher – start small, learn as you go, and don't be afraid to make mistakes.

What's the biggest mistake new investors make?

The biggest mistake is letting emotions drive investment decisions. The market is like a roller coaster – it has its ups and downs. Stay strapped in (stick to your plan) and don't jump off (make rash decisions) just because there's a dip.

Can I rely on financial news for investment advice?

Financial news can be a valuable source of information, but take it with a grain of salt. News can be sensationalized and may not always align with your investment strategy. Use it as one of many tools in your financial toolkit.

Is there such a thing as a 'safe' investment?

No investment is 100% safe – there's always some level of risk. But some investments, like government bonds or high-quality dividend stocks, are generally considered lower risk. Think of them as the comfy sneakers of the investment world – reliable, but not flashy.

Should I invest in cryptocurrency?

Cryptocurrency is the wild west of the investment world – high potential rewards but also high risks and volatility. If you're interested, start with a small portion of your portfolio and ensure it fits within your overall investment strategy.

How do I set realistic investment goals?

Set goals based on your financial situation, risk tolerance, and time horizon. Be specific and measurable, like saving for a down payment or building a retirement fund. Remember, it's a journey, not a sprint to the finish line.

Is it ever too late to start investing?

It's never too late to start! Like planting a tree, the best time was 20 years ago; the second-best time is now. Begin with what you can, focus on long-term strategies, and remember, investing is about playing the long game.

Final Thoughts: A No-Nonsense Farewell to Financial Fumbles

Well, folks, we've reached the end of our little financial escapade. It's been a ride, hasn't it? From debunking those pesky investment myths to taming the wild beast of market swings, we've covered a lot of ground. And let's not forget our deep dive into the quirky world of investor psychology – who knew our brains could be such drama queens when it comes to money?

Think of this book as your new financial playbook. It's not just a bunch of theories or complicated jargon that makes your head spin. It's a practical guide, a no-nonsense approach to investing. I've laid it all out in plain language – because let's face it, investing shouldn't be as complicated as rocket science.

Remember, smart investing isn't about following the latest fads or getting rich quick. It's about making informed decisions, understanding the risks, and yes, sometimes going against the grain. It's about being patient, persistent, and keeping your cool when everyone else is losing theirs.

Your journey in investing is as much about mindset as it is about money. It's time to look at finances differently – not as a tedious chore or a nerve-wracking gamble, but as an exciting opportunity to grow your wealth and secure your future. And hey, let's have some fun while we're at it, shall we?

So, what's next? It's time to take charge. Grab the bull by the horns, or the bear, depending on the day. Use the tools and insights you've gained from this book to carve your path in the world of investing. Make smart choices, learn from your missteps, and keep evolving.

Here's to you, the newfound investor, ready to conquer the financial world. May your investments be wise, your risks calculated, and your rewards plentiful. Go out there and make your mark – your financial freedom is waiting. Cheers to your success!